How to Barter, Buy, and Sell Like a Pro Today: The Best Investment You Can Make

I0504753

A guide to the low risk, high return, easy to break into world of bartering

Dominic Milam

Copyright-©-2019-by-Dominic-Milam-All-Rights-Reserved

Dominic Milam

Copyright-©-2019-by-Dominic-Milam-All-Rights-Reserved

"No part of this publication may be reproduced, distributed, or transmitted in any form or by any means, including photocopying, recording, or other electronic or mechanical methods, or by any information storage and retrieval system without the prior written permission of the publisher, except in the case of very brief quotations embodied in critical reviews and certain other noncommercial uses permitted by copyright law."

Table of Contents

Prologue

This book is for those of you seeking information on how to increase your personal wealth through the art of bartering. Through bartering you can increase your own wealth, without spending any significant amount of money. Bartering allows you to increase your personal wealth with no cap on how much you can earn. The risks are minimal, the payoff can be great, who wouldn't want to know how to be successful? This guide will show you different avenues as to how to break into the field, as well as personal tips I've learned in my own experiences. I will discuss the best tactics to employ to ensure you trade the right way, and walk away at the end of the day happy about your purchase and the knowledge you acquired to be able to continue making smart trade transactions in the future.

Why barter?

Everybody's heard the stories of Joe Schmo from Timbuctoo starting out with a pen. Through some magical mystical means, he's able to trade and ends up with goods far higher in value, be it an electronic item, a car, or even a house! What knowledge does Joe have that I don't? How did he make it seem so simple? Joe's secret was the art of bartering, or trading items or services he had available for other items or services. This is an amazing concept; in our society most people are aware that the continuous transactions we make throughout the day all have one thing in common – money. But money is not an endless resource. We have mortgages, insurance, car payments, and for a lot of people pursuing hobbies and pastimes is limited due to a lack of funds. With the skill of bartering, you can attain many items that you otherwise wouldn't have wanted to fork your hard-earned dollars over for. Want an ATV to ride around on? Maybe try trading that log splitter you have sitting unused in the back shed. Need parts to finish the car your restoring? Maybe someone with access to those parts could use your expertise in their own restoration, or you could provide some other service that they've been searching for. Whatever it may be, bartering has made it possible for thousands of people to acquire goods that they otherwise would not have been able to. This has succeeded for those looking for items to keep for their own use, as well as those looking for a side hustle, and to make some money for themselves.

We live in an age where this is easier than ever. The internet connects almost everyone and there are lots of useful sites and resources we can use to achieve our goals. Whether you are a

Facebook Marketplace fan, a Craigslist fanatic, or a user of applications like LetGo, there is a way for you to find others with items and services you could use. By the end of this short guide you will have many new tips on how to use these sites and your listings to your own advantage, as well as new skills in the personal transactions that take place through these avenues. How do I know this? Let me give you some background.

Personal Experience

I started bartering at the young age of 14. Just starting high school, I was the typical kid, involved in school, sports, extra-curriculars, even earned a little money on the side from small jobs like push mowing and gardening. But I was also fairly broke. I wasn't in need of anything, but I didn't have the funds to go out and buy fun items that many other students had around me. Wanting to be a successful young entrepreneur, I wondered how I could make some extra money over the summer to be able to spend, and I decided to grow what I was already doing, mowing lawns. The perfect summer job for a kid. I already had access to a push mower, but lacked the funds to purchase a riding mower. I began my quest by asking friends and family if they knew anyone that had a cheap riding mower for sale, but no one had one within my price range. I looked through ads in the local paper, looked at auctions, but I just couldn't find anything. That's when someone suggested to me, I should look on Facebook Marketplace. This was new to me, I had never heard of Facebook Marketplace, so I decided to give it a shot because I was out of ideas. It was like a brand-new world, from one small search I was able to see more ads then I had seen in two months from pounding the pavement, and it was all easily accessible! I ended up finding someone local that was throwing out a mid 80's cub cadet, a big iron beast of a mower that had stopped working for them. I had a bit of mechanical knowledge, I always enjoyed working on small engines, so I figured I would try and get it to work. The best part of this was that I got the mower for the crazy price of absolutely free! This was beyond exciting, and I pictured the stacks of money I would be making after my successful venture. I walked about a half mile to the address it was listed at and knocked on the door. After talking to the owner, he walked me around back and showed me where the mower was sitting covered in weeds. It had 4 good tires, so I thanked him and rolled it home. Over 2 weeks I tore it apart, cleaned it up, bought a $5 dollar fuel filter, and with some starting fluid and a battery charge it fired up and was ready to cut.

Now most bartering ventures aren't as lucky as this, the previous owner probably could have sold this mower for a buck or two if he really wanted, but plenty of ads that are listed online are just diamonds in the rough, waiting to be found. Whether it be someone that just wants an item gone, is in desperate need of funds, or doesn't know what they're selling, there are many a good deal to be found online, and this experience opened my eyes to the possibilities before me. I proceeded to use that mower for a year and a half before I started an actual job, and in that time, it never gave me an issue.

Now I had succeeded in two ways. I had made profit through using an item I had found online for free, and I had the working item I could sell or trade for its own value. I decided I'd try and trade it for something a little more fun, and I took back to Facebook Marketplace, as well as my local ads, and craigslist, because you can never have too broad of a search basis. I searched in the wanted ads on craigslist for riding mowers, using different keywords, and an ISO search in all the different categories on craigslist (ISO stands for in search of, it's a popular post by someone who is looking for something, but doesn't want to post in the wanted section of Craigslist). I couldn't find anybody who had any items for trade that I was interested in, so I started searching exclusively for items for trade, as well as barter listings, hoping to get lucky and find someone who just happened to be looking for a riding mower. I contacted many people, and if you become an avid user of online avenues for bartering and selling, you will learn that it will require a lot of contacting, calling, texting, and messaging, to get in contact with the right person with the right item in the right conditions. I found someone with a 3-wheeler that was running and driving, but was used on a farm and definitely showed its age. The guy was open to any and all trades, and so I texted him an image of the mower and asked if he'd be willing to trade. He was looking for trade value of around $500 and I figured I might be a bit low on the trade value side, but each item is worth something different to someone else and I had a bit of cash to add if it came to that. He responded quickly and low and behold, his mower had just quit and he needed something to mow the large yard around his house. I was in, the deal wasn't closed but I had an item that he needed, and I knew if he didn't get it from me, he'd have to spend the cash to get one anyway. We discussed and he agreed to trade the 3-wheeler for the mower if I threw in $100, this also included him driving an hour both ways to deliver the 3-wheeler and to take the mower. I had successfully completed my first barter, and made quite a profit doing so.

I knew I wanted to continue, so I looked for other items around my house. We had an old Snap-On tool chest that had been left in a barn for at least a couple decades, the paint was worn but it was in good shape. Doing some research, I found out how much gearheads love the Snap-On name, and I figured if I could spruce it up a little, I'd have something with decent value that I could use in future negotiations. I loved working on restoration projects myself, so I gave it some spray paint, lubed the shelf rollers, got some rubber mats for inside the shelves, and through the same process I was able to trade a previously unused low value item for a custom snowmobile valued around a grand. I proceeded to use this process extensively, searching as often as I could on the web. I traded both the snowmobile and the 3-wheeler for a little Dodge Ram pickup, and I traded that pickup for 2 Honda Goldwing motorcycles. I thought I had figured out the secret, I was ecstatic. That's when I got my first lesson in the complicated world of bartering.

Nothing comes with a guarantee, and when trying to start one of the Honda Goldwings, the belt broke and tore the motor apart. At that point it was really only good for parts, and so I ended up selling both motorcycles for $800. I was disheartened, as that was a bit of a financial setback, but I realized that I had put maybe $150 into this entire bartering escapade including the $100 from the deal with the 3-wheeler sale, and I had come out with a wealth of knowledge in personal barter and sales, as well as a good profit return. I proceeded to keep bartering and have had countless similar transactions ever since.

Tools of The Trade

At this point in the guide you're probably asking "What do I need to succeed in this endeavor?" "What tools do I have at my disposal to do this myself?" ... First, I'll start with some basics, to begin it would be of extreme usefulness to you to have access to both Facebook Marketplace as well as Craigslist. They are both great in their own right, and I frequent both of them. If you want to use Craigslist to search for items and contact sellers you don't need an account, but if you want to use it to list your own items it only takes a few minutes to create an account and I highly recommend it. To access Facebook Marketplace, you need an account to expand any item and get the sellers info, so I suggest creating a Facebook account if you haven't already, I'll assume you have one though. If that's the case, you need to go into your settings and enable Marketplace, it will allow an icon to appear in your taskbar that will bring you to the Marketplace location (Word of caution, you cannot access Marketplace if you are not of age 18. You also cannot access Marketplace if you've previously been suspended). I'll list some quick info of both sites.

Facebook Marketplace:

The home page of Facebook Marketplace has many helpful sections under categories like today's picks, newly listed near you, among many others. As you use Facebook Marketplace some sections are tailored more to items similar to your previous searches. You can search Marketplace with a general search, but you can also join what are known as "groups". These groups allow you to see items for sale or trade that are in a certain area, are in categories i.e. cars, houses, services, etc., as well as many other criteria. This is a great way to get into contact with others with similar interests as you, as well as to tailor the results you get when you search for items. Most groups have an administrator that approves you into the group. This is generally to make sure the people in the group are there for the right reasons, and not fake accounts. If you try to share items you find in groups, the people you share it with will have to have access to the group as well. Overall, Marketplace is a great option to be able to network and find many items close to you, as so many people use Facebook. It's also easier to keep in contact with buyers and sellers, and to build relationships that can help you down the road.

Craigslist:

Craigslist has been around for a while, and is a great site to find ads for various items. Craigslist is separated into states, and each state has various towns or areas that you can search. You can only search one area at a time, so for example if you live in the Lasalle, IL area, you would search for Lasalle IL Craigslist and use that link for your search. Craigslist does not offer a way to search multiple areas from the same tab, but at the bottom of the search page it will list similar items in nearby areas, and they offer many criteria to tailor your search like model years, price, condition, even make, model, cylinders, etc. for vehicles. It's a great way to get specific results in your set price range quickly. There are other sites online that allow you to search all of Craigslist's towns and areas, but they aren't supported by Craigslist and therefore aren't very streamlined.

There are many other ways to access the world of selling and trading, these are just two of my favorites. There are many applications being released that act similar to Marketplace and Craigslist allowing users to list their items. Users can search in a given area, but these apps lack the user base that Facebook and Craigslist have, so as not to become overloaded I'd suggest using Marketplace and Craigslist first. Another tool you should have depending on the items you are trying to trade for is a way to transport items. Some people are more than willing to deliver their items and take whatever you have for trade. But when you find the perfect item a longer distance away, or you find someone that doesn't want to drive, it will be really helpful to be able to transport items yourself. In some cases, you can negotiate lower prices or a better trade agreement if you mention that you will be the one doing the transportation. Be aware this also works in reverse, and a lot of people will try and charge you cash or try and get better trade terms if they have to drive. I have found you are a lot more likely to have to do the delivery yourself if you are the one responding to an ad. If someone responds to items you have listed, they tend to have the means to transport themselves, whether they bring it up or not. This isn't always the case, but more often than not this is how it works out. The final item I would suggest having is a little extra cash whenever you leave to go to someone that you are trading with. You may have to throw in some cash if they find something wrong with your product that wasn't discussed prior, or they could have something else of value to you that you would want to purchase along with your trade. You would be surprised how many times I've gone to trade for a tool or parts, and the person I'm trading with had a whole stash of items I could use that they have no use for. If you have a nice interaction with the other person, generally you can get a great deal on whatever other items you are purchasing. The way they view this transaction is just extra money on top of the trade value they were receiving already. You may be offering less than market value for the additional item, but the appeal of money right in front of you is hard to resist for many people. Be aware some purchasers may travel to you then start pointing out all kinds of minor flaws in whatever you had listed. If you were honest and inclusive in your advertisement, if you listed everything you knew about the item, and answered any questions they had, you are under no obligation to pay them more for driving to you. It is not your fault that they traveled without being fully set on completing the transaction for a used item. If you falsely advertised your item, if you intentionally left out important or damaging information, you are the bane of the bartering world and not only is it a crime, it is what turns a lot of people away from this kind of sale and you are hurting the market as a whole. But I believe you readers have the upmost integrity :)

How to Trade

Part I-

Step 1 of successful trading is finding the right items to trade for. There are many aspects to this but I will condense them as clear as I can. First and foremost, if you are trading to increase the value of your items, you need to be an expert in the field you are trading in. I'd suggest choosing two or three categories that you enjoy, and learning about many of the items in those categories. When you're an expert about the items you are purchasing, it acts almost like a security blanket during your transactions. It allows you to be near certain the trades your making will help you out in the long run. Making these categories something you enjoy will also help you stay motivated through the process. If you have, say, a tv, and you plan on trading up to a big fancy computer, try trading for exclusively electronic products. You will enjoy the items you trade for in the meantime to your main goal, and you are more likely to find someone willing to trade if your offering items similar to their own interests.

For me, I learned a lot about antique tools, outdoor off-road toys, and vehicles. This allowed me to know the actual value of the old handheld Snap-On tools and the Snap-On chest I had, as plenty of old gearheads approached me with lowball offers hoping I was someone just looking to get rid of an old rusty piece of metal. You don't want to be that person. You want to be the smartest person in your transaction, to know the ins and outs of the objects your looking at, you will feel confident, the buyer/ seller will know, and the transaction will go that much easier.

Many products also have certain models and years with known problems, and a short google search and some reading can save you time and headaches later on. I got a killer deal on a 4x4 Jeep Wrangler with all kinds of aftermarket modifications. I thought I had bought it for a great price, until I found out the rear frame rails had rusted out and it was a very expensive repair. Unknown to me, this was a known issue with some of the TJ era Wranglers, and it spurred me to learn more about the vehicles to protect me in the future. I was able to find a shop owner that was an expert on these Wranglers, and I was able to sell my Jeep, even with the major problem, to him for his own off-road build. He knew about the problem, but because of the killer deal I got in the first place he offered me even more than the purchase price, and I walked away unscathed. Another learning point, even though the original seller didn't need to list this vehicle so low to sell it, he did because he thought it would make an easier sale. This is technically illegal, and I could have pursued legal action if I had proof of him having knowledge of the failed frame integrity beforehand. Due to my own diligence this wasn't required, but the safest option is to completely avoid problems like these by knowing what to look for.

You also need to completely clarify the terms of your agreement before either of you travel to the sale. If you're talking about monetary private purchases, it's alright to have a general base number and work with it when you meet in person. But in bartering transactions with no flexibility, it needs to be absolutely clear that if both parties are satisfied with each other's products the sale will be for solely trading those items, with no room for negotiation when you meet up. This saves time, headaches, and gas money.

Part II-

The second part to successful trading is the personality you portray throughout the sale, and the interactions you have with the buyer/seller. There have been many books written on this subject, and I will give you my personal viewpoint. It's been proven that people are more willing to be open to conversation, and in turn negotiation, with someone that has a pleasant demeanor. This includes common courtesies such as letting them know when you're close to meeting up, saying please and thank you, a handshake and a smile when you first meet. This applies even before you meet, when you're messaging about the items. I've contacted multiple people about possible trades and decided not to proceed with the transaction for the sole reason that I didn't appreciate their tone on the phone, or even over text. When someone inquires about an item, don't just respond with a one-word answer. Make sure to respond completely in full sentences, and answer any questions they may have asked. One of my biggest pet peeves is when you inquire about an item and ask for pictures and the seller sends you a few photos, and nothing else. When you don't answer all my questions, it makes it apparent you don't value the fact I'm possibly interested in your item. You don't seem interested in the transaction and this turns me away from continuing it.

When showing someone the item you have for trade, allow them to completely look it over and don't be afraid to voluntarily give any and all information on it. Tell them about all the maintenance you've done on the vehicle, all the upgrades you've done to it, but also tell them about any problems you think stick out or they should know about. For one, this lessens their fear that you are trying to hide something from them. If the transaction goes through, they are less likely to contact you later and complain about problems they were not informed of. It also allows them to trust you, and for most people trust is a large factor in private negotiations. It may even help you score a better deal if the person can tell that you truly care about the transaction and are not trying to screw them over.

A large part of this type of hobby is networking, you have to have good people skills and be willing to talk and interact. When you display confidence, and can speak your mind pleasantly, beyond getting your points across and helping for a smoother transaction the buyer/seller will respect you more for it. Many future trades and transactions can be with previous buyers/sellers, they have an interest in the same hobbies you do, they already partake in the bartering world by meeting with you, and if the trade is successful they will have some respect for you and the pleasant transaction they already had. They also might have knowledge and resources they are willing to share with you that could prove invaluable. They may know about a swap meet near you that you had no idea about, but has killer items. They might know someone with a cheap set of aluminum heads for the 350 small block you have sitting in your garage. Part of these transactions is building a temporary friendship for the duration of the meeting and portraying your best self, and if you're lucky that friendship could continue after the transaction.

Part III-

The third and final part of this process is closing the deal. This is the part most people fear, but also look forward too. This is where you can make or break the time and money you spent researching, contacting countless people, finding the right ad, and getting to the point of sale. After you both have looked over the items and have determined they meet your requirements is when you start talking about price. You should already have set terms if this a barter trade, and therefore you can complete the transaction and leave happy with your trade.

If money is involved, there should be a ballpark price that was discussed prior to meeting up. You both may present flaws that were seen with each other's items that either of you think should affect the price. Beware the buyer that starts pointing out every little scratch, speck of dirt, or scuff on an old and well used item. These people are either trying way too hard to get you to lower the price, or they have no idea how the actual used market works and believe they can buy a brand-new item with the huge markdowns that used items have. If they start pointing out flaw after flaw and offer an extreme lowball, it might be better to just cut your losses and walk away from the transaction. As hard as you try to weed out these time-wasters before getting to the point of sale, some of them will find a way to weasel into your schedule and you just have to accept that these people will not be willing to compromise at a price that is satisfactory to both of you. If you are dealing with someone who is not this way and you are honestly going back and forth on price, try not to be the first person to give a number. It is a lot easier to respond to a price than it is to set where the bar is at. Many times, I have had a number I was thinking I'd like to settle on in my head, and because I waited for the seller to speak first, they started with a price lower than I was willing to settle on! At that point you can decide to proceed at that price or respond with a number a little bit lower. If they offer a number better than what you were expecting I'd suggest just going with what they suggested. It's not worth it to try and possibly squeeze a few more bucks out of them, and risk offending them with a lowball offer, or on the flip side, too high a selling price. Once you give the appearance of someone who is just trying to scam them out of some more money, you instantly lose their trust and it's quite possible they may walk away from the sale right then and there. I've been on both ends of these kinds of transactions and it's not pleasant.

Once you agree on a price, congratulations. You've successfully bought, sold, or traded for the item you were searching for. Go have fun with your new purchase... or wash, rinse, and repeat the same process until you end up with what you're truly after. The hardest part of the sale is reading the seller, and being able to respond in an appropriate manner. If you keep these general guidelines in mind, keep a pleasant demeanor, and can arrive at a price or terms that work for the both of you, then you can successfully barter or buy and sell anything, and it'll just get easier with practice.

Conclusion

I hope you learned some valuable information from this book. These strategies have worked and continue to work for me, and I wish you the same luck that I have experienced. If you enjoyed this book, please leave a review on Amazon or share this book with your friends and family, it would be greatly appreciated!

Thank you,

Dominic Milam

Dominic Milam

Dedication-

"To the honest man/woman trying to make their time and money count for all its worth. Never stop the hustle."

www.ingramcontent.com/pod-product-compliance
Lightning Source LLC
Chambersburg PA
CBHW031509210526
45463CB00003B/1149